Floating

by **Dana Meachen Rau**

Reading Consultant: Nanci R. Vargus, Ed. D.

Marshall Cavendish
Benchmark
New York

Picture Words

 balloons

 boat

 bubbles

 clouds

 duck

 ducklings

 frog

 ice

 leaf

 penguins

 sails

 sky

 tube

 water

3

Many things float in the ⬭.

Many things float on ⬭.

 float in the .

Hold on to the string.

 float in the .

 look pink at sunset.

 float in the air.

You can make a lot of them.

A  floats on .

The blow in the wind.

 floats on .

 take a ride.

A  floats on .

A 🐸 takes a ride.

A  floats on .

Her  follow her.

You can float in .

A ⭕ keeps you up.

Words to Know

blow (bloh)
to make air move

follow (FOL-oh)
to go after

wind moving air

Find Out More

Books

Rau, Dana Meachen. *Fluffy, Flat, and Wet: A Book About Clouds*. Minneapolis, Minnesota: Picture Window Books, 2006.

Saunders-Smith, Gail. *Ducks and Their Ducklings*. Mankato, Minnesota: Pebble Books, 2004.

Walker, Pamela. *Welcome Books: Boat Rides*. Danbury, Connecticut: Children's Press, 2000.

Videos

Gordon, Tom. *See How They Grow: Pond Animals*. Sony Kids' Video.

There Goes a Boat. KidVision.

Web Sites

Boat Safe Kids
http://www.boatsafe.com/kids/index.htm

Mystic Seaport: The Museum of America and the Sea
http://www.mysticseaport.org

National Air and Space Museum: Full of Hot Air
http://www.nasm.si.edu/exhibitions/gal109/LESSONS/TEXT/HOTAIR.HTM

About the Author

Dana Meachen Rau is an author, editor, and illustrator. A graduate of Trinity College in Hartford, Connecticut, she has written more than one hundred books for children, including nonfiction, biographies, early readers, and historical fiction. She likes to float in a lake near her home in Burlington, Connecticut.

About the Reading Consultant

Nanci R. Vargus, Ed.D, wants all children to enjoy reading. She used to teach first grade. Now she works at the University of Indianapolis. Nanci helps young people become teachers. She spent six days floating down the Colorado River on a white water raft.

Marshall Cavendish Benchmark
99 White Plains Road
Tarrytown, NY 10591-9001
www.marshallcavendish.us

Library of Congress Cataloging-in-Publication Data

Rau, Dana Meachen, 1971–
Floating / by Dana Meachen Rau.
      p. cm. — (Benchmark rebus)
Summary: Simple text with rebuses explores things that float, from balloons and boats to penguins and clouds.
Includes bibliographical references.
ISBN-13: 978-0-7614-2315-7
ISBN-10: 0-7614-2315-X
1. Rebuses. [1. Air—Fiction. 2. Water—Fiction. 3. Rebuses.] I. Title. II. Series.
PZ7.R193975Fab 2006
[E]—dc22
        2005032987

Editor: Christine Florie
Editorial Director: Michelle Bisson
Art Director: Anahid Hamparian
Series Designer: Virginia Pope

Photo research by Connie Gardner

Rebus images provided courtesy of *Dorling Kindersley*.

Cover photo by Chad Ehlers/*Index Stock Imagery*

The photographs in this book are used with permission and through the courtesy of:
Getty: p. 21 Photodisc Blue; *Corbis:* p. 5, p. 7 Grace/zefa; p. 9 Charles Krebs; p. 11 Will & Deni McIntyre; p. 12 David Brooks; *Picturequest:* p. 13 Pam Ostrow; *Minden Pictures:* p. 15 Tui de Roy; p. 17 Fred Bravenclam; p. 19 Konrad Wothe.

Printed in Malaysia
1 3 5 6 4 2